Caught in the Quiet

BOOKS BY ROD McKUEN

Rod McKuen

CAUGHT
IN THE
QUIET

STANYAN BOOKS

RANDOM HOUSE

In love or out of love we are suspended as
in a limbo created by the presence of
or the lack of someone else.

I never like to analyze what I am writing
or what I have written, and so in
commenting on this particular work I can
only say that it has come from a recent
limbo that has given me more than all the
limbos of my small lifetime.

—R.M. March 1970

Caught in the Quiet

Caught in the quiet
off on our own
coming together
staying alone...

one

Not by the sun's arithmetic
or my own
can I make the days
go fast enough.
Yet there are those
who beg God daily
for an extra hour.
I wish for them no solitude,
no time apart from what they love,
and let them have their extra hour.

Caught in the Quiet

two

In becoming part of someone else
   you lose yourself
      and
that's the very least that happens.
Lucky are the ones who gain a language
or stumble on a system not yet tried
while they're giving up
what little independence
there is left in life.

Rod McKuen

three

What I've gained
from being with you
(besides a belly
and a deeper beard),
I couldn't say—
but any need for knowing
anyone but you
   is what I've lost.

Caught in the Quiet

four

Out of the sad mistaken belief
that as a man I must behave
as all men do.
I've turned my back
a time too often.
God,
help me keep
a resolution that I make today:
not to walk head high
even one more time
past someone I can help.

Rod McKuen

five

Every time we say hello
to some new encounter
we're on our way
toward goodbye.
Some distance
from the actual phrase
but moving toward it all the same.
The distance between those two words
becomes a little less
as we grow older.
Be aware then
that tomorrow
is only tomorrow.
There is nothing to fear
except the coming of another day.
But two against a winter morning
are sure to claim one more victory
over chance and trouble.
If I seek your eyes
I'll do so with my own eyes only.

Caught in the Quiet

six

Perhaps I'm not too far away
from the time when people see
the way I look at them
for what it means.
Not want, but need.
How much safer to want:
women don't expect
so much from you then.

Rod McKuen

seven

There are some wars
a man should never be afraid to lose.
One is the loss that comes from loving
whether in the lightning
    or the dark.

Caught in the Quiet

eight

Love,
being the right hand of God,
should be dealt with courteously.
And fireworks that fizzle in July
should not be held accountable in August.
I will not scold you
just because you changed your mind,
though I'll admit a jealousy of curtains
that just now separate your face from mine.

Rod McKuen

nine

The lifetime I have left
I open up to you
to tread upon
and travel through.

You pave the road
        I'll follow,
You build the bridge
        I'll test it first.

Caught in the Quiet

ten

My dog likes oranges
but he'll eat apples too.
Like me,
he goes where the smiles go
and I'd as soon lie down
with sleeping bears
as track the does by moonlight.

Don't trouble me
with your conventions,
mine would bore you too.

Rod McKuen

Straight lines are sometimes
difficult to walk
and good for little more
than proving we're sober
on the highway.

I've never heard
the singing of the loon
but I'm told he sings
as pretty as the nightingale.

My dog likes oranges
but he'll eat apples too.

Caught in the Quiet

eleven

You said
I'll always be there
and you are.

Sometimes
the distance
that you keep
is as difficult
for me to bear
as proximity would be
to anyone I didn't care for.

Rod McKuen

twelve

Trust me
and I'll do
good things for you
even if to make you happy
means to leave you
to yourself.

Caught in the Quiet

thirteen

I promised I would call
I used to do that often
and meant it at the time
as I meant to answer letters
and take the dogs out walking
the same hour every day.

I didn't call because I didn't
and because a promise
I might keep
that leads you nowhere
would be unkinder
than those good intentions
that grow dim.

Caught in the Quiet

fourteen

You love me
with your patience
how hard you work
and how you try.

I give back as my share
(in this contract not yet made)
    just myself
That seems so little.

Rod McKuen

fifteen

If you like apples
then I'll carry home an orchard.
If sky is to your liking,
I'll bundle up the skies of summer
so you never need to know
the winter evening anymore.

I like the fire
and so I wait for winter nights.
Apples I can take or leave . . .

Your body like your mind
has need of going over
and I intend to be a journeyman
    of your soft skin,
for years to come.

Caught in the Quiet

sixteen

My sister had three dolls,
Imogine, Diane and Vera.
One day I operated on them
and removed their cry boxes.
Now they don't cry anymore.

But people really cry;
a good thing to remember
in taking love in stride,
in taking love at all.

Rod McKuen

seventeen

Often I wonder
why we go on running.
There are
so few things pretty
left in life to see.

That is until tomorrow
when the crocus jumps up
back in California courtyards,
and you become
my back rest
and my English bible.

Caught in the Quiet

eighteen

The moonrise
and the sunfall
are visible
to any blind man
with eyes enough
to feel the outline
of another blind man's breath.

Caught in the Quiet

nineteen

I accept the fact
that love is love,
though I understand it
not at all.

I understand
your belly though
and tulips in a jar
and only that
I'd make of you
exactly what you are.

Rod McKuen

twenty

I mustn't crowd you
I know that
your laugh on Christmas eve
should be enough—
though we both know it isn't.

I try to look the other way
when you walk in a room
but, Jesus, was there ever
such a magnet as your face?

Compulsions
stronger than the will of God
make me want to kill your smile
before another man can see it.

Caught in the Quiet

twenty-one

There were no seagulls here today
warm winds have blown them
off to warmer sands.
To Spain or Greece where there are rocks
and all the caves are
plentiful with clams.

Lying by the sea I watch the *giogoli*
track the ladies down the beach
thinking all the while
of Muir Woods redwood trees.
Green fields and sheep dogs,
red poppies seen from train windows.

You wouldn't like the beach today
the flags are all so tattered
the kites are all too few.

Rod McKuen

You'd be like me
wondering how I came to be here
not troubled but not happy.

God I hate this waste of time.
I should be chopping wood
or raking leaves
or home in bed
with all those tired dreams
I saved so carefully
for such days as these.

I could count the ceiling cracks
and feed the animals
their Crackerjacks.

Caught in the Quiet

Though I feel spent
let down and done,
trying to slow down is not so easy
when your thoughts still
hang on yesterday.

Dodging pigeons in the square
while five-piece combos
grate my ears,
I'm restless all day long.

Apart I am
and much alone.

Rod McKuen

Did you feel the same
while riding home to California?
What were your thoughts and
secret wishes?

I'll tell you this—
you've earned the right to rest awhile
and occupy your time
with just the breakfast dishes.

I know what's happening to us
and I know why.
Outside myself I stand
looking back in abject amazement.

Caught in the Quiet

twenty-two

Loving
is the only sure road
out of darkness,
the only serum known
that cures self-centeredness
or puts it there.

I have said I love your body
as I love my own.
I mean not just the contours
and the weight that shifts to me
but that I would protect you
from the robber baron
as I would protect myself.

Rod McKuen

twenty-three

I am
and I am not
a kind man
when it comes to loving.

Help me up
if I fall down
and prop my head
against the sink
if need be.

I am sick of sunshine
when you lie in bed
beside me.
But when you venture
through the door
I need the daylight desperately.

Caught in the Quiet

twenty-four

I know
I'm coming to the coda
as I know all waltzes stop.

If we stay at distance
five years more is all I need
If you hold me
fifteen minutes should be plenty.

Rod McKuen

twenty-five

There are no tangibles
but how you taste
and I've near forgotten that.

The only valuable I own
is a victory over alcohol
while putting you to bed
one early morning.

Caught in the Quiet

twenty-six

In loving you
I've held back no reserve
and so I've nothing left
to give tomorrow's lover
when you go.

Rod McKuen

twenty-seven

And now
I lay me down to sleep
and not alone.

Dear God
I do believe in you
how else could such a thing
come true for me?

Caught in the Quiet

twenty-eight

Please help me.
Passing thirty
sick on silence
I'm dying of indifference
every day.

I do not ask your counsel
merely the covenant
of your arms,
even silence from you
if you're still with me.

It's the silence by myself
that doesn't heal the wounds.

Rod McKuen

twenty-nine

The spring has seen us both
side by side and singing.
Did you think I'd dare
to leave you walking lonesome
into someone else's summer?

If it's someone else you need
I'll take you to him
and find my way
back home alone.
But I'll not have you
going aimlessly away
whatever be your liking.

Caught in the Quiet

thirty

So close upon a narrow bed
that we are indivisible
I blot out everything
but your brown eyes.

And with the safety valve
of you at home
I last a single hour
in the marketplace.

Rod McKuen

thirty-one

Given the choice
getting inside somebody
even with a smile
makes more sense than always
looking through the glass
at someone else's candy.

A sweet tooth
doesn't always need
the richest cake.
Sometimes cookies
and a glass of milk will do.

Caught in the Quiet

thirty-two

Smiles
are passports
through the desert
and visas to
all alien countries.

I am your family
and your winter fire
let me do your crying
and you can make
my smiles for me.

Rod McKuen

thirty-three

Bare-bellied
in the bedroom
or coming from the bath
you look like every invitation
to every party I dreamed of
that never came.

I salute the sensibility
of your stomach
and pledge allegiance to it
as my only flag.

Caught in the Quiet

I know
that I'm preoccupied
with backs and bellies,
I'm told that all the time—
but God's face and Syracuse
are too far out of reach
to be of any use at all.

Rod McKuen

thirty-four

Man may love
his fellow man now
and roses too,
mini minds in maxi skirts
and all things green.

The liberation
has come so far
that I can show
my love for you
without your laughter
as a rude reply.

People in the streets must know
for when we pass
the passageways are clear.

Caught in the Quiet

thirty-five

I am to love you
I'm sure of that
this month of March.
Could I go back before November
and take a different road
I might.

But I'd have missed
your face against my own
that first December night
and turning on by turning
to look back at you
every time I went away.

Then coming
up the hill again
to face you head on
as you buzzed me through
your Spanish doorway.

Rod McKuen

thirty-six

Saturday
keep secrets
that Sunday
never could.

I came
to love you.
I wonder
if you knew
or know.

Caught in the Quiet

I wonder
if you looked on me
so gently
just because
you knew
looks were all
I'd get from you
all that you
could give.

Stringing me along
isn't what you're guilty of
not stringing me along
might cause
your citizen's arrest.

Rod McKuen

thirty-seven

You may puzzle at me
when I tell you
that your not loving me
is the most love
that I ever had.

But anyone who's
given in to loving
will know and understand.

Caught in the Quiet

ROD MCKUEN was born in Oakland, California, in 1933, and grew up in California, Nevada, Washington and Oregon. He has traveled extensively both as a concert artist and as a writer. In the past three years his books of poetry have sold in excess of three million copies in hardcover, making him not only the best-selling poet of this age but probably every other era as well. In addition, he is the composer of more than a thousand popular songs, several film scores, including *The Prime of Miss Jean Brodie* (for which his song received an Academy Award nomination). Artists such as Frank Sinatra, Petula Clark, Glenn Yarbrough, Rock Hudson, Claudette Colbert and Don Costa have devoted entire albums to his composition.

His major classical works, *Symphony #1, Concerto for 4 Harpsichords and Orchestra* and *Concerto for Guitar and Orchestra,* have been performed by leading American symphony orchestras as well as those in foreign capitals of the world.

Before becoming a best-selling author and composer, Mr. McKuen worked as a laborer, radio disc jockey, newspaper columnist and as a psychological-warfare script writer during the Korean War.

He is currently writing screenplays based on his first two books of poetry and is about to make his debut as a film director.

When not traveling, he lives at home in California in a rambling Spanish house with a menagerie of sheep dogs, cats and a turtle named Wade.